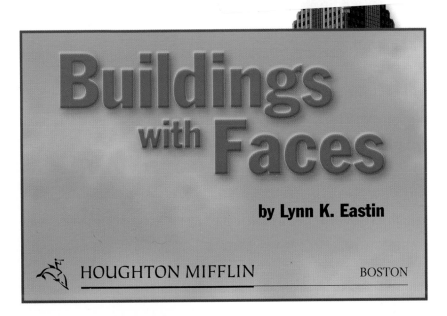

Buildings with Faces

by Lynn K. Eastin

HOUGHTON MIFFLIN   BOSTON

PHOTOGRAPHY CREDITS
Cover © John Dakers/Eye Ubiquitous/Corbis; **1** © Ingram Publishing/SuperStock; **2** © Ingram Publishing/SuperStock; **3** © David Hodges/Alamy; **4** © Arcaid/Alamy; **5** © Scala/Art Resource, NY; **6** © Bill Ross/ Corbis; **7** © Arco Images/Alamy.

Printed in China

ISBN 10: 0-618-90005-5
ISBN 13: 978-0-618-90005-3

56789 0940 16 15 14 13

4500404667

Two Prudential Plaza is the fifth tallest skyscraper in Chicago, Illinois. It has 64 floors and a total height of 995 feet. The building's straight edges and rectangular faces give it a sleek look. The pyramid at the top of the building supports an 80-foot spire. Two Prudential Plaza was built in 1990, and it has won several awards for its architecture.

Read·Think·Write What is the shape of the pyramid at the top of this building, a square pyramid or a triangular pyramid?

Two Prudential Plaza

The Hotel Nacional de Cuba has stood in Havana, Cuba, since 1930. Rectangular prisms make up the shape of this beautiful hotel. However, on top of the hotel are two towers that have a different shape. Each tower has eight sides. Imagine a room with eight walls and a flat ceiling and floor. That room forms an octagonal prism. The roofs on the towers show yet another three-dimensional figure. They are pyramids because they have triangular faces that come to a point, also called a vertex.

Hotel Nacional de Cuba

The Nakagin Capsule Tower in Tokyo, Japan, was built in 1970. It was the first tower of its kind to really be used. Each room is a rectangular prism called a capsule. A room measures 2.3 m × 3.8 m × 2.1 m. This means each room has a volume of about 18.35 cubic meters, which is a very cozy space! A circular window in each capsule allows people to see outside. Only four bolts attach each capsule to the concrete center. The capsules were built so they could be taken down or moved if necessary.

Read·Think·Write What makes the capsules in the Nakagin Capsule Tower rectangular prisms rather than cubes?

Nakagin Capsule Tower

Triumphal Arch of Augustus

In 29 B.C., the Triumphal Arch of Augustus was built. The ruins of the arch still stand in Rimini, Italy. When the arch was complete, it had three entrances. The middle entrance was vaulted. That means the top part had a curved surface. The two side entrances were flat at the top. Today, only the middle entrance remains. On each side of the arch stands a column that has the shape of a cylinder.

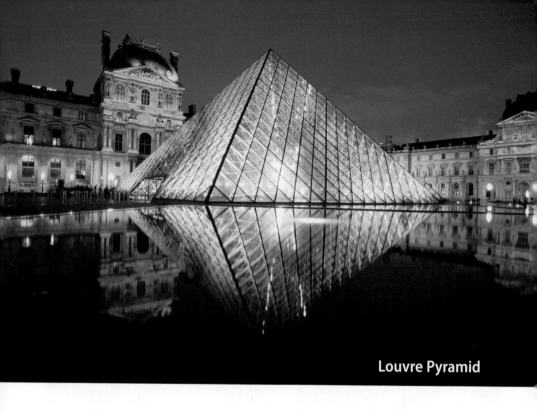

Louvre Pyramid

As you walk up to the front of the Louvre Museum in Paris, France, an interesting sight meets you: a steel and glass pyramid. Built in 1989, the pyramid stands 71 feet tall. Its clear walls allow sunlight to stream into the museum's front hall. Many people were unhappy with this pyramid. They felt that it did not match the look of the rest of the museum.

Read·Think·Write How many triangular faces does the Louvre pyramid have? What shape is the base?

When is an art museum more art than museum? When it is the Frederick R. Weisman Art Museum in Minneapolis, Minnesota. The museum building on the University of Minnesota campus was completed in 1993. The building combines curved and flat faces and straight and rounded edges. The outside is covered in stainless steel. Its shiny surface reflects the sun and the river below.

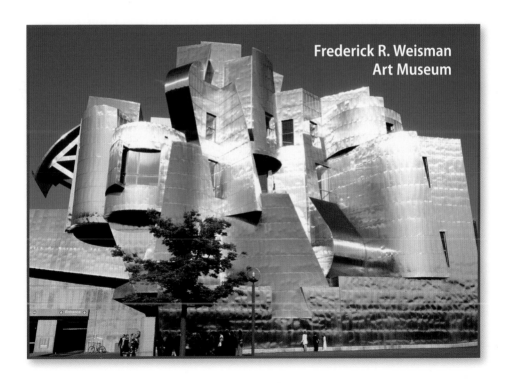

Frederick R. Weisman
Art Museum

1. **Visualize** Imagine using two building blocks to make a house. The house has four equal sides. The roof comes to a point, and each face of the roof is a triangle. What is the shape of the block you used for the roof?

2. The front entrance of the White House in Washington, D.C., has four tall columns. What three-dimensional figure do the columns have?

3. What is the shape of a room with a triangular ceiling and a matching triangular floor?

Activity

Using blocks, clay, and other materials, design and build a building. Include three of the following figures in your design: rectangular prism, pyramid, cone, cylinder, cube.